FAMILY ADVENT DEVOT

Counting to CHRISTMAS

Written by GAIL PAWLITZ

Illustrated by

EVA VAGRETI

CONCORDIA PUBLISHING HOUSE · SAINT LOUIS

To my dear children (Loren, Aaron, Jen, Rachel, Jessica, Josh, and John), and all parents, who faithfully teach their children about Jesus— His birth, death, and reign.

Manufactured in Guangdong, China/033411/415892
4 5 6 7 8 9 10 11 12 13   31 30 29 28 27 26 25 24 23 22

Introduction

How exciting! Christmas is coming. And you are getting ready.

Advent is the season of the Church Year that comes right before Christmas. It is a time of preparation, a time to focus on our need for a Savior and on God's response to that need by sending His very own Son to be our Savior.

For children, these are days of excitement and wonder. Lights, decorations, carols, trees, and cookies. Gifts, Santa, and Jesus. Children wonder how these things fit together. Through simple routines—reading Scripture, lighting candles, singing carols, setting up the nativity—they can find hope and comfort in Jesus. This resource will acknowledge their wonder and guide them through the maze of sights and sounds to celebrate Jesus' birth. It will help you keep faith a priority in your lives.

God bless you as you use this resource, *Counting to Christmas*. God bless you as you, like your child, wonder at God's amazing gift, His own dear Son, your Savior, Jesus Christ.

—The author

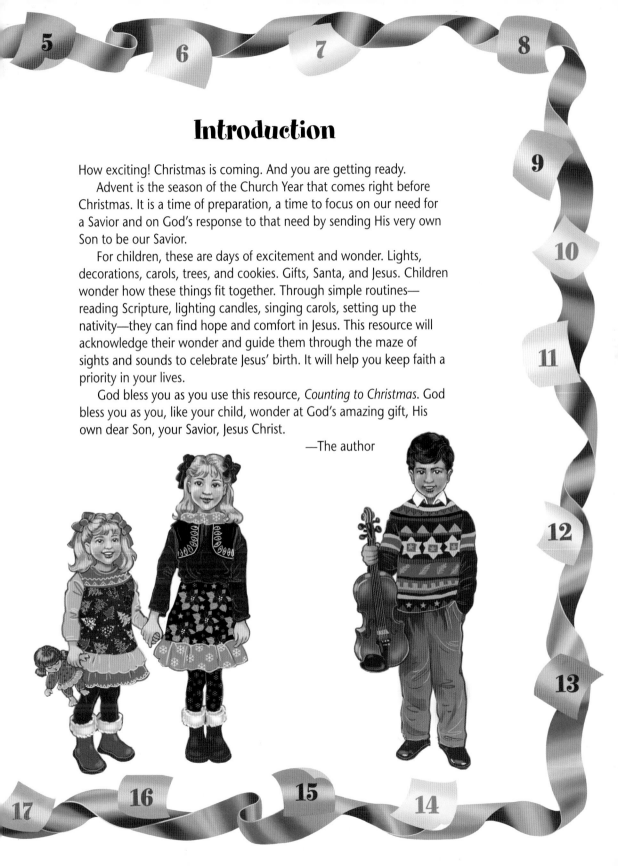

I wonder, how did the **real story of** Christmas begin?

Day 1

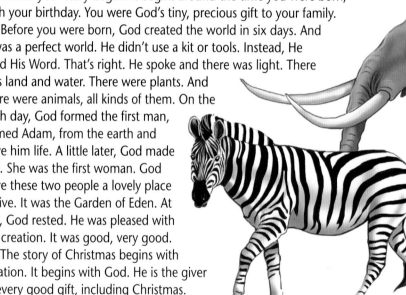

How does your story begin? It begins around the time you were born, with your birthday. You were God's tiny, precious gift to your family.

Before you were born, God created the world in six days. And it was a perfect world. He didn't use a kit or tools. Instead, He used His Word. That's right. He spoke and there was light. There was land and water. There were plants. And there were animals, all kinds of them. On the sixth day, God formed the first man, named Adam, from the earth and gave him life. A little later, God made Eve. She was the first woman. God gave these two people a lovely place to live. It was the Garden of Eden. At last, God rested. He was pleased with His creation. It was good, very good.

The story of Christmas begins with creation. It begins with God. He is the giver of every good gift, including Christmas.

Say it

"In the beginning, God created the heavens and the earth."

Genesis 1:1

Do it

Name something God created that starts with the first letter of your name.

Pray it

Take turns thanking God for each thing you named.

I wonder, what happened in the Garden of Eden?

Day 2

Where did you go today? What happened? Was it a good day or a bad day?

Adam and Eve had good days in the Garden of Eden. But one day was very bad for them and for us too.

That day, the devil tempted them. He told them it was okay to eat of the tree of the knowledge of good and evil. But that wasn't true. God had told Adam and Eve to stay away from that tree. But they did not. Adam and Eve ate. They disobeyed God. They sinned.

God knew what happened. He punished the devil. And He sent Adam and Eve out of the garden for their own good. But God also gave them hope and a super-wonderful promise. He said one day He would send a Savior. The Savior would do everything just right. The Savior would also win a victory over sin, death, and the lying devil.

God's promise day was a good day for you too. Do you know whom God sent? That's right. Jesus! And you can learn more about Him in God's Word.

Say it

"All have sinned and fall short of the glory of God."

Romans 3:23

Do it

Draw pictures that show something good that happened to you today. Share them. Thank God for His goodness.

Pray it

Thank God for His promise and for sending Jesus to be your Savior from sin, death, and the devil.

I wonder, how did the people after Adam and Eve hear about **God's** promise?

Day 3

What do you know about your family? Have you seen baby pictures of your parents? heard stories about your relatives? It's a fact. Someone in your family came before you. You descended from someone.

Long ago, God spoke to a man named Abraham. He told Abraham he would have a big family. In fact, God told Abraham to go outside his tent and count the stars if he was able. God promised Abraham many descendants (people in his family), as many as the stars in the sky. God also promised to bless all nations through Abraham's family. It may have seemed hard to believe since Abraham was one hundred years old and his wife, Sarah, was ninety. But Abraham had faith in God's promises.

Did God keep His promise? Of course! It took a lot of years, but it happened. And Jesus was one of Abraham's descendants.

As you wait for Christmas to come, look at the stars. Count them if you can. Listen to God's promises in His Word. Think of Jesus, Abraham's descendant and your Savior.

Say it

"[The Lord said to Abraham,] 'In you all the families of the earth shall be blessed.'"
Genesis 12:3

Do it

At night, look at the stars. Find a bright one. Then tell how God has blessed your family.

Pray it

Ask God to bless your family as you hear the promises in His Word.

I wonder, what does the word Emmanuel mean?

Are you looking forward to someone coming? A visitor? God's people were looking forward to the coming of the Savior God promised.

Long ago, Isaiah, God's prophet (a person who speaks God's words for God), said God was coming to visit. Isaiah said a virgin would give birth to a Son. That Son would be the Savior God promised.

God's Son was to be named Emmanuel. That name means God with us. Jesus is our Emmanuel too. He is God with us.

First, God sent Jesus as a baby. Years later when Jesus was grown up, Jesus suffered and died on the cross for our sins. Now through faith and in our Baptism, God comes to us in His Word through His Spirit. And someday, Jesus will come again!

As you get ready for Christmas, sing the hymn "O Come, O Come, Emmanuel." Rejoice! God sent Jesus to be your Savior.

Say it

"'Behold, the virgin shall conceive and bear a son, and they shall call His name Immanuel' (which means, God with us)."

Matthew 1:23

Do it

Wave your hands and sing, "Rejoice! Rejoice! Emmanuel Shall come to thee, O Israel!"

Pray it

Thank God for sending Jesus to be your mighty Savior and loving friend.

Day 5

I wonder, what do wreaths have to do with Christmas?

Draw a circle in the air with your finger. Do it again. Round and round you go. A true circle has no ending. It will go on forever. God will go on forever. He is eternal.

Wreaths are in the shape of a circle. They are often green. They remind us that God gives eternal life. God sent His Son, Jesus, to earth to live without sin. And then Jesus suffered on the cross and died for our sins. Through the gift of faith in Jesus, we have the gift of eternal life. We also have the forgiveness of sins.

As you light candles on an Advent wreath or see lovely Christmas wreaths hanging about, thank God that He sent His Son, Jesus. Draw a circle with your finger and say, "God gives eternal life to me!"

Say it

"*God gave us eternal life. . . . Whoever has the Son has life.*"

1 John 5:11–12

Do it

Decorate a wreath and hang it. Then look for other wreaths. Where did you spy them?

Pray it

Thank God that He has given you eternal life through faith in His Son, Jesus Christ.

Day 6

I wonder, who was St. Nicholas?

Did you put your shoes by the door last night? Did you hope to find some coins in them this morning? Or maybe some candy? Perhaps you thought St. Nicholas would visit. Some people celebrate St. Nicholas Day in those ways.

Nicholas was a real person who lived long ago. He was a pastor in Myra, now in the area around Turkey. It is said that Nicholas loved children. He was kind and giving to those in need because He loved God.

God is kind and giving. He gives us lots of good gifts, including our bodies and families. He gives food and places to live. He gives us pastors like St. Nicholas too. He gives us things we can share with others in need.

On this day, many people give gifts. They talk about the good works of Nicholas of Myra. On this day, we can thank God for St. Nicholas and others who do works of charity. We can give gifts to charity because God gave His only Son to be our Savior.

Christmas gift-giving started with God. He gave us His best gift. He gave us Jesus.

Say it

"Oh give thanks to the Lord, for He is good."

Psalm 118:1

Do it

Choose to do an act of charity; help someone else.

Pray it

Ask God to give you grace to help the poor and helpless.

I wonder, did Bethlehem have Christmas trees?

Day 7

Do you have a Christmas tree?
Does it have lights on it?

The Bible doesn't tell us about Christmas trees. But it does tell us about other trees. The tree of the knowledge of good and evil was in the Garden of Eden. Adam and Eve ate fruit from it. They disobeyed God, and sin came into the world.

Another tree in the Bible is the tree of the cross. Because of Jesus' death there for our sins, we are forgiven. We have the gift of eternal life. The Bible also tells us the tree of life grows in heaven. It has wonderful fruits and healing leaves.

So you may wonder how Christmas trees started. No one is sure. But years ago, a man named Martin Luther cut down a fir tree. He took it home and put real candles on it. The lights twinkled like the stars over Bethlehem.

Today, many people put up trees and lights. If you do, remember the trees in the Bible. Thank God He sent His Son for you.

Say it

"[Jesus] bore our sins in His body on the tree, that we might die to sin and live."
1 Peter 2:24

Do it

Look for drawings of the tree of life.

Pray it

Thank God for the tree of the cross and for the tree of life in heaven.

I wonder, what does it mean that Jesus is a branch from a stump?

Day 8

Stumps.

They are a tree part still in the ground after a tree is cut down. Below the stump are roots. Often, a stump looks dead. But sometimes, a new branch comes out of a stump.

Long ago, God's prophet Isaiah foretold the coming of the Savior. He said the Savior would be a branch from the stump of Jesse. The words *branch* and *stump* are picture language. They mean the new Savior-King would be born from the family of Jesse, a family that no longer had any ruling kings.

The new Savior-King would bear fruit. That means the new King would do all that God desires. He would not sin. He would be righteous.

Now the people had hope. The Savior-King would live and rule in a spiritual kingdom. We have hope in Jesus too. He lives and rules in our hearts. He is our Savior-King.

Say it

"There shall come forth a shoot from the stump of Jesse, and a branch from his roots shall bear fruit."   Isaiah 11:1

Do it

Take a picture of a stump. Print it. Draw a new branch growing from it.

Pray it

Ask Jesus to rule in your heart and mind.

I wonder, how do **love** and **Christmas** go together?

Day 9

How do you show love to other people? Do you give them a "squeezy" hug and say, "I love you"? Do you buy them a gift? Do you draw a picture? Words and actions go together.

How does God show His love for us? He shows it with words and actions. At Christmas, God's words of promise came true. He acted. In the Bible, God tells us He sent His Son as a gift to be our Savior from sin. Years later on the cross, Jesus acted. He died. He paid for our sins, for our unloving thoughts, words, and actions. God forgives us through faith in Jesus. He gives us His victory over sin, death, and the devil!

Yes, love came down from heaven to earth at Christmas. We can rejoice! We can sing, "God loves me dearly, loves even me."

Say it

*"**God so loved the world, that He gave His only Son, that whoever believes in Him should not perish but have eternal life.**"*

John 3:16

Do it

Sing the hymn "God Loves Me Dearly."

Pray it

Thank God for Jesus, His loving gift.
Then ask Him to help you share God's love.

I wonder, is
Jesus a real king?

Day 10

Kings wear crowns. Kings have scepters. Kings rule kingdoms. They are wise and fight battles.

Is Jesus a real king? Yes. He was born a king. He came to save His people from sin.

Once, Jesus wore a crown of thorns. Soldiers put a robe on Him. Then they put Him on a cross to die. On that cross, Jesus won a battle for us. He beat our enemies—sin, death, and the devil. And on Easter, Jesus showed He was alive, the winner.

Do you wonder where King Jesus is now? God's Word tells us He is ruling in the hearts of His children. He is ruling the universe. On the Last Day, King Jesus will come again. He won't be in a manger. He will come on the clouds with the sound of a trumpet. And He will take us to be with Him!

Say it

"[Jesus] is the radiance of the glory of God and the exact imprint of His nature, and He upholds the universe by the word of His power."

Hebrews 1:3

Do it

Make crowns to put on your Christmas tree.

Pray it

Ask King Jesus to rule in your heart and someday take you to be with Him.

I wonder, how could **baby Jesus be called a key?**

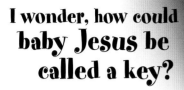

Day 11

Keys have power. You already know how important they are. Keys can open doors to good places and treasured things. They can also lock up bad people and keep out evil.

Jesus is God's key. He has awesome power. God sent Jesus to earth as a man on a mission. He came to unlock the chains of sin. Jesus came to win a victory over the powers of death and the evil devil. To complete His mission, Jesus had to live perfectly and die for our sins. And Jesus did it. Then He rose victorious on Easter. No stone could lock Him in the grave. And because we have faith in Jesus, we share His victory.

Now you can rejoice! Jesus came to be your key. He came to set you free. He came to unlock heaven for you.

Say it
"And I will place on his shoulder the key of the house of David. He shall open and none shall shut; and he shall shut, and none shall open."
Isaiah 22:22

Do it
Talk about Jesus' work as a key as you hang one on your Christmas tree.

Pray it
Thank God for sending His Son to rescue you from sin and open heaven's door for you.

I wonder, how could **baby Jesus be the Prince of Peace?**

Day 12

Waah! Waah! Waaaah! Babies cry when they are hungry. Babies cry when they are bored. Babies cry when they are tired. Crying is baby talk.

When we say baby Jesus is the Prince of Peace, we are not saying He never cried.

Here is what it means. Long ago, God promised to send a Savior who would pay for the sins of all people. That peace required perfect living and then death.

Jesus is the prince of God in God's heavenly kingdom. God sent His Son, the prince, to earth on a mission. Jesus lived perfectly. He died in our place. Jesus brought peace between God and folks like us.

This world is not a peace-filled place. Today, tomorrow, and until Jesus returns, there will be troubles. But while God's children have troubles, we still have peace. In God's Word, we have Jesus, our heaven-born Prince of Peace. He brings us life and salvation.

Say it

"For to us a child is born, to us a son is given; and the government shall be upon His shoulder, and His name shall be called Wonderful Counselor, Mighty God, Everlasting Father, Prince of Peace."

Isaiah 9:6

Do it

Memorize Isaiah 9:6.

Pray it

Ask the Prince of Peace to rule in your life.

Day 13

I wonder, what about the light and dark of Advent?

You probably noticed. In December, darkness comes earlier each day. No more staying out late to play. And the morning light comes later. No more getting up to sunshine and breakfast. It seems that darkness and light are having a battle. And it seems that darkness is winning. But don't worry. It's not.

You probably noticed something else. In Advent, we light more and more candles. Light is winning. We sing songs and hymns that look forward to the Savior's birth. We remember that Jesus overcame the darkness of sin and powers of death. He is the light of the world.

So light Advent candles. Light the Christmas tree. Light up the night-light. Rejoice. Jesus is coming. He is the winner over all your dark enemies. He takes away the sadness of your sin. He gives you songs of gladness.

Say it

"Again Jesus spoke to them, saying, 'I am the light of the world. Whoever follows Me will not walk in darkness, but will have the light of life.'"
John 8:12

Do it

Light a candle in a dark room or on an Advent wreath. Sing an Advent hymn.

Pray it

In Baptism, God made you a new person. Ask Him to help you live by His light.

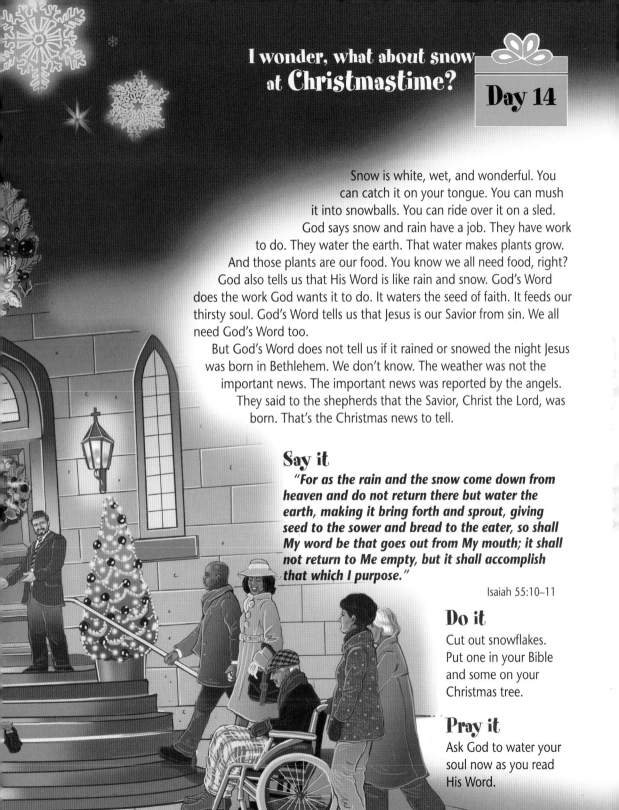

I wonder, what about snow at **Christmastime?**

Snow is white, wet, and wonderful. You can catch it on your tongue. You can mush it into snowballs. You can ride over it on a sled. God says snow and rain have a job. They have work to do. They water the earth. That water makes plants grow. And those plants are our food. You know we all need food, right? God also tells us that His Word is like rain and snow. God's Word does the work God wants it to do. It waters the seed of faith. It feeds our thirsty soul. God's Word tells us that Jesus is our Savior from sin. We all need God's Word too.

But God's Word does not tell us if it rained or snowed the night Jesus was born in Bethlehem. We don't know. The weather was not the important news. The important news was reported by the angels. They said to the shepherds that the Savior, Christ the Lord, was born. That's the Christmas news to tell.

Say it

"For as the rain and the snow come down from heaven and do not return there but water the earth, making it bring forth and sprout, giving seed to the sower and bread to the eater, so shall My word be that goes out from My mouth; it shall not return to Me empty, but it shall accomplish that which I purpose."

Isaiah 55:10–11

Do it

Cut out snowflakes. Put one in your Bible and some on your Christmas tree.

Pray it

Ask God to water your soul now as you read His Word.

I wonder, what about the **songs** called **Christmas carols?**

Day 15

You probably know all the words to "Jingle Bells." Singing about jingling bells is fun, but the words don't tell the real meaning of Christmas.

Carols are Christian songs that tell the real meaning of Christmas. The words of "Silent Night" proclaim that "Christ, the Savior, is born!" The words of "Away in a Manger" ask the little Lord Jesus to be with us forever. And in "Joy to the World," we proclaim that the Lord is come. He is King. He came to rule with truth and grace. These hymns help us rejoice because the Savior is born, the very Savior God promised to rescue us from sin, death, and the devil. They tell how our sadness has been turned to gladness.

You may not understand words like "Gloria in excelsis Deo," but you can sing them. You can rejoice because the Savior is born. You can adore Him, Christ the Lord.

Say it

"Sing to the Lord, all the earth! Tell of His salvation from day to day."

1 Chronicles 16:23

Do it

Sing each person's favorite Christmas carol.

Pray it

Pray in song, thanking God for the gift of His Son, the Savior of all.

I wonder, are **happiness** and **Christmas joy** the same thing?

Day 16

Happiness comes from the outside in. It comes to you through God's blessings. You make Christmas cookies. You are happy. You eat them. You are even happier. Your friend plays with you. You are happy. Your friend spends the night. You are even happier.

Joy comes from the inside out. It comes as God's gift through Jesus.

On that first Christmas night, the angels brought the shepherds "good news of great joy." Jesus, the Savior, was born!

Jesus was born to be our Savior too. He comes inside us through the blessings of Baptism. He comes inside us through His Word. There, we hear the Good News that He died to win a victory over death. We hear that He paid for our sin—the wrong we think, say, and do. There, we hear that Jesus has a forever home for us in heaven.

Happiness is great, but real joy is better. It lasts forever.

Say it

"And the angel said to [the shepherds], 'Fear not, for behold, I bring you good news of great joy that will be for all the people. For unto you is born this day in the city of David a Savior, who is Christ the Lord.'" Luke 2:10–11

Do it

Make a joy ornament to put on your Christmas tree.

Pray it

Ask the Holy Spirit to give you joy no matter what happens to you.

I wonder, what does John's **birth** have to do **with Christmas?**

Have you ever been in a play? This time of year, boys and girls act out the Christmas story. Someone is Joseph. Someone is Mary. Others are angels, shepherds, and even Wise Men. But hardly anyone is ever John.

Who was John? He was Jesus' cousin. He was a baby when Jesus was born. Zechariah and Elizabeth were his parents. An angel brought the baby news to Zechariah while he was working in the temple. The angel said that John would have a special job. John would help people prepare their hearts and lives for the coming of the Lord. John would get them ready for Jesus.

God gives you His Word. And He sends people who help you prepare your heart and life for Jesus' coming. They take you to church. They help you learn your part in the Christmas play. They talk with you about sin and Jesus' forgiveness. They say, "Get ready! Jesus is coming!"

Say it

"The angel said to him, 'Do not be afraid, Zechariah, for your prayer has been heard, and your wife Elizabeth will bear you a son, and you shall call his name John. And . . . he will be great before the Lord.'"

Luke 1:13–15

Do it

Thank your parents, pastors, and teachers for helping you to get your hearts and lives ready for Jesus' coming.

Pray it

Ask God to bless those who preach and teach the Good News that Jesus is coming.

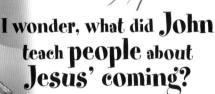

Day 18

I wonder, what did John teach people about Jesus' coming?

Bulldozers and road graders have a huge job. Excavators have a big job too. These machines make roads. They move rocks and push soil. They smooth bumps and fill holes. They prepare a highway for people to come and go.

John was not a bulldozer or loader. But John had a big job. He helped people get ready for Jesus' coming. He told them to move away from sinning. He told them to be sorry for the sinful things they did. He told them to repent and change. These acts would prepare the way for Jesus to come.

Right now, you are preparing for Christmas. You are decorating a tree and buying presents. That's great. But if you want to get your heart ready for Jesus, listen to God's Word. Listen to John's message. Prepare the way. Confess your sins. Say you are sorry for them. Know God forgives you for Jesus' sake. Live as a child of God.

Say it
"**Prepare the way of the Lord; make straight in the desert a highway for our God.**"   Isaiah 40:3

Do it
Confess your sins. Imagine Jesus pushing them far, far away.

Pray it
Ask God to help your family prepare your hearts for the coming of Jesus.

I wonder, what about Jesus' mother, Mary?

You probably know that Mary was Jesus' mother, but you may not know how she found out she would be His mother. One day, the angel Gabriel showed up in Nazareth where Mary lived. Gabriel said Mary would carry baby Jesus in her womb. The angel said God would make it happen. He said Jesus would be the Son of God.

Whoa! That was a surprise. You see, Mary was already betrothed to Joseph. But Mary didn't say no. Instead, she answered in faith. She said, "Behold I am the servant of the Lord; let it be to me according to your word" (Luke 1:38).

This Christmas, God's Good News comes to you. It comes as you read or hear God's Word. It comes to you in His Sacraments. And God calls little you to live by faith in your own special way. Like Mary, you can say, "Behold, I am the servant of the Lord."

Say it

"Mary said, 'Behold, I am the servant of the Lord; let it be to me according to your Word.'"

Luke 1:38

Do it

Set up a nativity set.

Pray it

"O holy Child of Bethlehem,
Descend to us, we pray;
Cast out our sin, and enter in
Be born in us today." Amen.

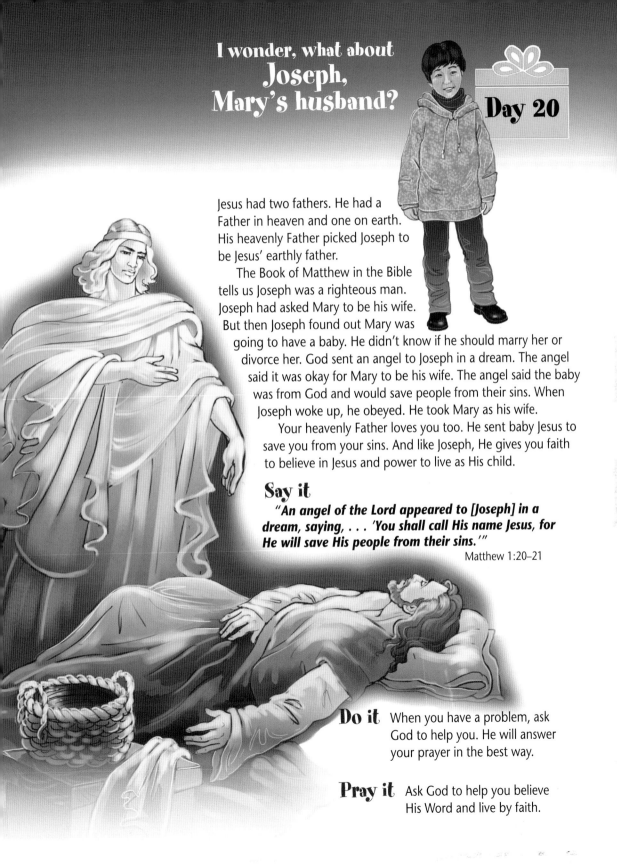

I wonder, what about
Joseph, Mary's husband?

Day 20

Jesus had two fathers. He had a Father in heaven and one on earth. His heavenly Father picked Joseph to be Jesus' earthly father.

The Book of Matthew in the Bible tells us Joseph was a righteous man. Joseph had asked Mary to be his wife. But then Joseph found out Mary was going to have a baby. He didn't know if he should marry her or divorce her. God sent an angel to Joseph in a dream. The angel said it was okay for Mary to be his wife. The angel said the baby was from God and would save people from their sins. When Joseph woke up, he obeyed. He took Mary as his wife.

Your heavenly Father loves you too. He sent baby Jesus to save you from your sins. And like Joseph, He gives you faith to believe in Jesus and power to live as His child.

Say it
"An angel of the Lord appeared to [Joseph] in a dream, saying, . . . 'You shall call His name Jesus, for He will save His people from their sins.'"
Matthew 1:20–21

Do it
When you have a problem, ask God to help you. He will answer your prayer in the best way.

Pray it
Ask God to help you believe His Word and live by faith.

I wonder, who tells angels what to do?

Day 21

You know what messages are, right? And you know messengers bring messages. But did you know that angels are God's messengers? He tells them what to do.

One night, an angel appeared to shepherds who were out in the fields near Bethlehem. The angel had this message: "Fear not, for behold, I bring you good news of great joy that will be for all the people. For unto you is born this day in the city of David a Savior, who is Christ the Lord" (Luke 2:10–11). Then that angel told the shepherds where to find the baby. He would be wrapped in swaddling clothes and lying in a manger. Then a multitude of angels showed up praising God. What a sight!

God's messages about Jesus are for you too. His Word shows you just where to find the Savior. He is there in the manger! Worship Him, Christ the Lord!

Say it

"And suddenly there was with the angel a multitude of the heavenly host praising God and saying, 'Glory to God in the highest, and on earth peace among those with whom He is pleased!'"
Luke 2:13–14

Do it

Sing "Hark! The Herald Angels Sing."

Pray it

Thank God for those who bring you the message that Jesus, the Savior, is born.

I wonder, who picked Bethlehem as the place Jesus was born?

Where were you born? No one could have guessed the place you would take your first breath years before it happened. But that's not true about Jesus.

About seven hundred years before that first Christmas night, the prophet Micah said Jesus' birth would happen in Bethlehem. So God picked Jesus' birthplace. Through God's power, Micah foretold that a ruler would come from Bethlehem. That ruler would lead His people and "be their peace" (Micah 5:5).

Bethlehem? But Mary and Joseph didn't live in Bethlehem. You may wonder why they were there. Here's why. The ruler Caesar Augustus was taking a census. And so the young couple had to go there to register. So now they were in the right place for Jesus' birth.

This Advent season is the right time to read God's Word and remember that the holy Child of Bethlehem was born for you too. He came to take away your sin and live with you.

Say it
"But you, O Bethlehem, . . . from you shall come forth for Me one who is to be ruler in Israel, whose coming forth is from of old, from ancient days."
Micah 5:2

Do it
Sing "O Little Town of Bethlehem."

Pray it
Pray for babies born today. Ask God that they, too, might know the love of God through Christ Jesus, our Christmas Savior.

I wonder, how did Jesus end up in a manger?

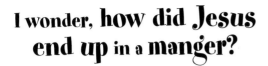

Day 23

Do you ever travel? Do you stay in a hotel? If so, your bed there may not be like your bed at home. It might be smaller or even bigger.

Long ago just before Jesus was born, Mary and Joseph were traveling. They were in the crowded city of Bethlehem. There was no room in the inn for the couple. So Mary and Joseph settled in with the animals. Then that night, Jesus was born. His mother, Mary, wrapped Him in swaddling cloths. Then she laid baby Jesus in a manger. Imagine, the Son of God asleep in a feeding trough. What a humble bed for the Savior of all.

Tonight when you go to bed, snuggle up in your blankets. Thank God for the birth of baby Jesus. Thank God He is your Savior. Thank God that through faith in Jesus, you are royalty; you are a child of God.

Say it

"And she gave birth to her firstborn son and wrapped Him in swaddling cloths and laid Him in a manger, because there was no place for them in the inn."

Luke 2:7

Do it

Donate baby items to a charity.

Pray it

Ask God to bless and keep you as His child by faith, wherever He leads you.

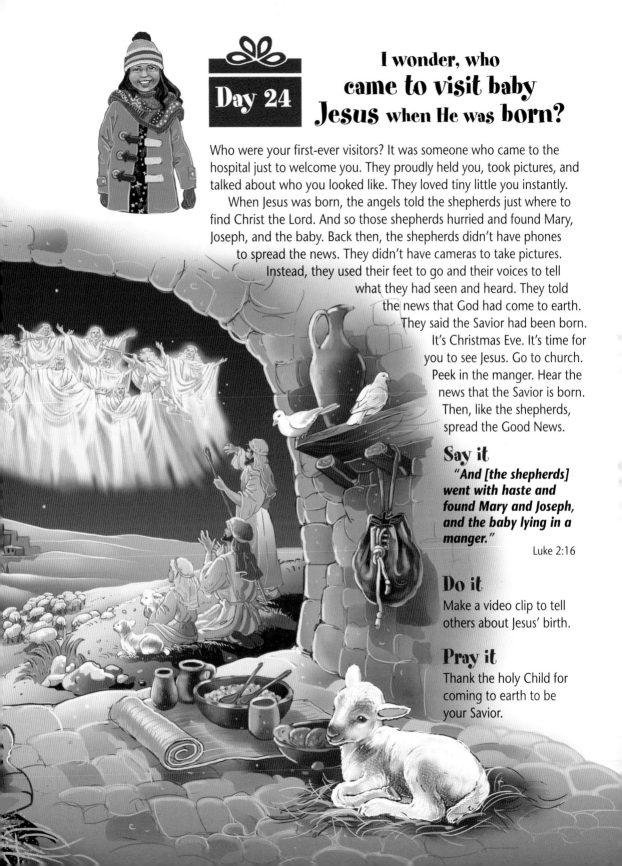

Day 24

I wonder, who came to visit baby Jesus when He was born?

Who were your first-ever visitors? It was someone who came to the hospital just to welcome you. They proudly held you, took pictures, and talked about who you looked like. They loved tiny little you instantly.

When Jesus was born, the angels told the shepherds just where to find Christ the Lord. And so those shepherds hurried and found Mary, Joseph, and the baby. Back then, the shepherds didn't have phones to spread the news. They didn't have cameras to take pictures. Instead, they used their feet to go and their voices to tell what they had seen and heard. They told the news that God had come to earth. They said the Savior had been born. It's Christmas Eve. It's time for you to see Jesus. Go to church. Peek in the manger. Hear the news that the Savior is born. Then, like the shepherds, spread the Good News.

Say it

"And [the shepherds] went with haste and found Mary and Joseph, and the baby lying in a manger."

Luke 2:16

Do it

Make a video clip to tell others about Jesus' birth.

Pray it

Thank the holy Child for coming to earth to be your Savior.

I wonder, what gift can I give Jesus?

Day 25

When you were born, you were God's gift to your family. How do you celebrate your birthday? Do you get gifts? Does your family sing to you? Do you eat cake?

When Jesus was born, He was God's gift to Mary and Joseph and also to all people! Jesus was sent to live perfectly. And He was sent to die. Many years after His birth, Jesus would die on a cross to pay for the sins of the world.

Jesus was born as God's gift to you too. He was born to live, die, and rise for you. Through faith in Him, you are a son or daughter in His family. Your sins are forgiven. You have a home in heaven.

How can you celebrate Jesus' birth? What gift can you give Him? You can go to church and hear God's Word. There, you can see the Savior. You can adore Him, Christ the Lord.

Say it

"And the Word became flesh and dwelt among us, and we have seen His glory, glory as of the only Son from the Father, full of grace and truth."

John 1:14

Do it

Sing "O Come, All Ye Faithful."

Pray it

Ask God to be present with you now and to fill your life with His grace and truth.

I wonder, who led the Wise Men to Jesus?

Epiphany

Have you ever used a map to get somewhere special? Or have you had someone lead you somewhere?

January 6 marks the time long ago when God used a star, a dream, and His Word to guide the Wise Men to Jesus. You've probably seen pictures of these men in fancy robes, wearing crowns, and riding on camels.

These Wise Men didn't use a map. They didn't have a guide. Instead, God led them with a special star. It guided them to Jerusalem first and then on to Bethlehem.

After searching for many days, these men saw the newborn King, gave Him gifts, and worshiped Him.

Today marks another day when God is guiding you to find Jesus. He does this through His Word and Sacraments. They point the way to Him. Through them, you can see who Jesus is, offer Him gifts, and worship Him—the Savior of all.

Say it

"When they saw the star, they rejoiced exceedingly with great joy. And going into the house, they saw the child with Mary His mother, and they fell down and worshiped Him."

Matthew 2:10–11

Do it

Make craft-stick puppets of the Wise Men and tell the story from Matthew 2.

Pray it

Ask God to let Jesus be the star of your life.

God Loves Me Dearly

God loves me dearly, Grants me salvation,
God loves me dearly, Loves even me.
Therefore I'll say again: God loves me dearly,
God loves me dearly, Loves even me.

He sent forth Jesus, My dear Redeemer,
He sent forth Jesus And set me free.
Therefore I'll say again: God loves me dearly,
God loves me dearly, Loves even me.

Hark! The Herald Angels Sing

Hark! The herald angels sing, "Glory to the newborn King;
Peace on earth and mercy mild, God and sinners reconciled!"
Joyful, all ye nations, rise, Join the triumph of the skies;
With the angelic host proclaim, "Christ is born in Bethlehem!"

O Little Town of Bethlehem

O little town of Bethlehem, How still we see thee lie!
Above thy deep and dreamless sleep The silent stars go by;
Yet in thy dark streets shineth The everlasting light.
The hopes and fears of all the years Are met in thee tonight.

O holy Child of Bethlehem, Descend to us, we pray;
Cast out our sin, and enter in, Be born in us today.
We hear the Christmas angels The great glad tidings tell;
O come to us, abide with us, Our Lord Immanuel!

O Come, All Ye Faithful

O come, all ye faithful, Joyful and triumphant!
O come ye, O come ye to Bethlehem;
Come and behold Him Born the king of angels:
O come, let us adore Him, O come, let us adore Him,
O come, let us adore Him, Christ the Lord.

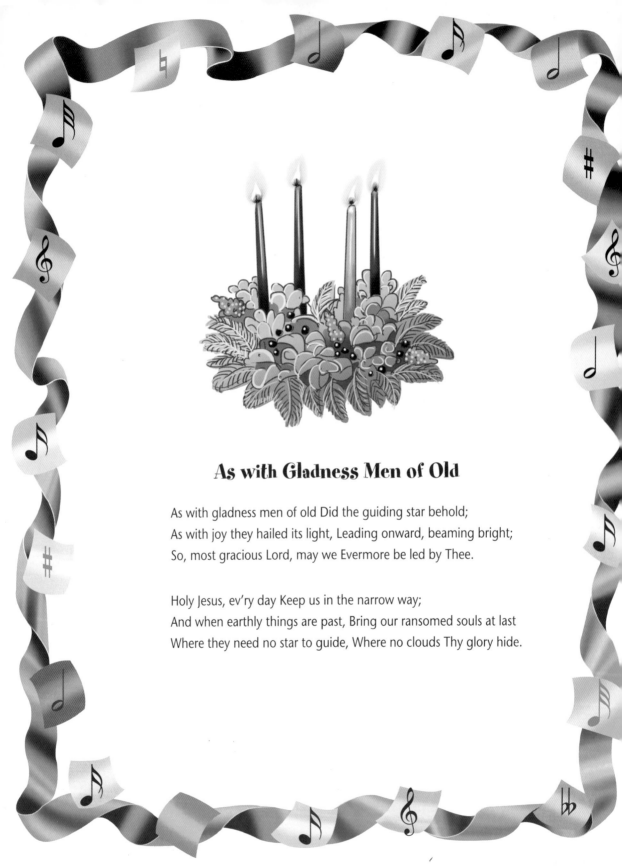

As with Gladness Men of Old

As with gladness men of old Did the guiding star behold;
As with joy they hailed its light, Leading onward, beaming bright;
So, most gracious Lord, may we Evermore be led by Thee.

Holy Jesus, ev'ry day Keep us in the narrow way;
And when earthly things are past, Bring our ransomed souls at last
Where they need no star to guide, Where no clouds Thy glory hide.